Bradley N. M

David L. Ranum, Luth

COMPUTER SCIENCE:

PYTHON

Programming Language

JONES AND BARTLETT PUBLISHERS

Sudbury, Massachusetts

BOSTON   TORONTO   LONDON   SINGAPORE

World Headquarters
Jones and Bartlett Publishers
40 Tall Pine Drive
Sudbury, MA 01776
978-443-5000
info@jbpub.com
www.jbpub.com

Jones and Bartlett Publishers Canada
6339 Ormindale Way
Mississauga, Ontario L5V 1J2
CANADA

Jones and Bartlett Publishers
International
Barb House, Barb Mews
London W6 7PA
UK

Jones and Bartlett's books and products are available through most bookstores and online booksellers. To contact Jones and Bartlett Publishers directly, call 800-832-0034, fax 978-443-8000, or visit our website www.jbpub.com.

Substantial discounts on bulk quantities of Jones and Bartlett's publications are available to corporations, professional associations, and other qualified organizations. For details and specific discount information, contact the special sales department at Jones and Bartlett via the above contact information or send an email to specialsales@jbpub.com.

6048

Production Credits
Acquisitions Editor: Tim Anderson
Production Director: Amy Rose
Editorial Assistant: Laura Pagluica
Production Assistant: Jamie Chase
Manufacturing Buyer: Therese Connell
Marketing Manager: Andrea DeFronzo
Composition: Northeast Compositors
Cover Design: Timothy Dziewit
Cover Image: © Joseph/ShutterStock, Inc.
Printing and Binding: Kase Printing
Cover Printing: Kase Printing

ISBN-13: 978-0-7637-4316-1
ISBN-10: 0-7637-4316-X

Printed in the United States of America
10 09 08 07   10 9 8 7 6 5 4 3 2

The Python Programming Language

After studying this chapter, you should be able to:

- Describe the interactive Python environment.

- Describe the structure of a Python program.

- Implement selection statements using *if* and *if-else* structures.

- Implement iteration using *for* and *while* structures.

- Use the built-in collection classes (string, list, and dictionary).

- Use files for input and output.

- Construct a function and use parameters and return values.

- Understand how Python supports object-oriented programming.

1.1 What Is Python?

Python is a modern programming language that is both easy to learn and easy to use. It is ideal for beginning programmers, as it combines a clear, simple syntax with support for a powerful set of built-in control structures and data types. Python is also used by many professional programmers to write complex software systems.

The Python programming environment can be used interactively. After starting Python, the prompt (>>>) appears, indicating that Python is waiting for you to enter a command. Once you enter a command, the Python environment evaluates (interprets) this command and then displays the result. This sequence of events is known as the read-evaluate-print cycle. The following session shows the Python interpreter in action after it is started from a UNIX command prompt:

```
$ python
Python 2.4.1 (#2, Mar 31 2005, 00:05:10)
[GCC 3.3 20030304 (Apple Computer, Inc. build 1666)] on darwin
Type "help", "copyright", "credits" or "license" for more
information.

>>> print "Python programming is fun!"
Python programming is fun!
>>>
```

It is often more practical to write an entire Python program. A program is simply a number of Python commands (also called statements) that are stored together in a file. The entire program can then be executed all at once. For example, assume that the following Python program is stored in the file spider.py (Python file names should end with .py):

```
#This program prints out a nursery rhyme
#Here are some useful action phrases:
verb1 = "went up"
verb2 = "down came"
verb3 = "washed"
verb4 = "out came"
verb5 = "dried up"

#Build each line of the rhyme

firstline = "The itsy bitsy spider " + verb1 + " the waterspout"
secondline = verb2 + " the rain and " + verb3 + " the spider out"
```

```
thirdline = verb4 + " the sun and " + verb5 + " all the rain"
fourthline = "and the itsy bitsy spider " + verb1 + " the spout again"

#Print the first 3 lines followed by a semicolon
#Print the fourth line followed by a period

print firstline + ";"
print secondline + ";"
print thirdline + ";"
print fourthline + "."
```

Now, if we start the Python interpreter and provide the file name containing the Python program, the interpreter will execute all of the statements in order from top to bottom. Note that Python assumes that the file is in the current directory. If this is not the case, we can give the complete path name for the file. The output of the program can be seen below:

```
$ python spider.py
The itsy bitsy spider went up the waterspout;
down came the rain and washed the spider out;
out came the sun and dried up all the rain;
and the itsy bitsy spider went up the spout again.
$
```

An additional option in the Python interpreter allows you to execute a program and then remain in interactive mode. By remaining in the interactive mode, you can evaluate variables that appear in the program. In the following example, we execute the spider.py program as before and use the interactive mode to check some of the variable values used to build the rhyme sentences.

```
$ python -i spider.py
The itsy bitsy spider went up the waterspout;
down came the rain and washed the spider out;
out came the sun and dried up all the rain;
and the itsy bitsy spider went up the spout again.
>>> verb1
'went up'
>>> firstline
'The itsy bitsy spider went up the waterspout'
>>>
```

Before moving on, let's examine a few elements in this Python program. First, notice that some of the lines start with a "#" character. This symbol is known as a comment marker. All of the text on the line following this marker is meant for the reader and will be ignored by the Python interpreter. Comments are often used to make programs easier to understand.

Second, each statement starts at the same left-hand margin. Python uses this indentation level as a guide for which statements should be executed together. We will see different indentation levels later as we consider a variety of control structures.

We will now turn our attention to describing the basic Python constructs. Many of the early examples can be explained by looking at and describing interactive sessions. We encourage you to start your Python interpreter and experiment as we explore the Python programming environment.

1.2 Python Data

Python supports the object-oriented programming paradigm, which means that data is central to the problem-solving process. In Python, a class describes what a piece of data looks like as well as which operations the data can perform. Data items are often referred to as data objects (or, more simply, as objects). Each object is an instance of either a Python-defined class or a user-defined class (described later in this chapter).

Primitive Numeric Classes

We begin our study of data by considering the primitive classes that can be used to describe numeric data. Python offers three built-in numeric classes: integer, long integer, and floating point. Long integers are capable of representing very large integer values and have an "L" character at the end of their value. Floating-point numbers include decimal points. Evaluating a numeric data object simply returns that object.

```
>>> 16
16
>>> 5.75
5.75
>>> 239384162897958
2393841628958L
>>>
```

Numbers come with a standard set of arithmetic operations (referred to as "methods" in the object-oriented paradigm) that allow you to construct arithmetic expressions. The operators +, -, *, /, and ** can be used to perform addition, subtraction, multiplication, division, and exponentiation, respectively. When two integers are divided, an integer result is returned—a process known as integer division. The remainder after integer division can be computed using the % operator. At least one of the operands must be a floating-point value for the result to also be a floating-point value. Arithmetic operations that result in large values automatically return long integers.

The session below demonstrates the arithmetic operations and includes comments for further explanation. Remember that the Python interpreter will ignore these comments.

```
>>> 5+7             #Addition
12
>>> 4*6             #Multiplication
24
>>> 8/3             #Integer division since 8 and 3 are
integers
2
>>> 8.0/3           #Floating-point division
2.6666666666666665
>>> 8%3             #The remainder after dividing 8 by 3
2
>>>2**5             #2 raised to the fifth power
32
>>> 3**50           #Large integers are automatically long
717897987691852588770249L
>>>
```

When an arithmetic expression contains more than one operation, the order of evaluation is important. The rules of precedence dictate this order. In Python, operations involving the exponentiation operator are done first. Next, multiplication and division are performed, followed by addition and subtraction. To change the order in which these operations are carried out, we can insert parentheses in the expression.

```
>>> 5*6+7
37
>>> 5*(6+7)
65
>>> (2+3)*(4+5)
45
>>> 2**3 + 3**2
17
>>> (2+3)**2
25
>>>
```

To help us with more complex arithmetic, Python provides a math library. Before you can use this library, however, you must make it available to the Python environment by executing an *import* statement. Once the library has been imported, you can use its functions and constant values in any expression combined with any other operators you like. In the following examples, the last one uses the result of one math library function (radians) to provide a value to another math library function (sin).

```
>>> import math
>>> math.sqrt(34)
5.8309518948453007
>>> math.pi
3.1415926535897931
>>> math.sqrt(34) + math.sqrt(65)
13.89320964314385
>>> math.sin(math.radians(90))
1.0
>>>
```

A very useful feature of the interpreter environment is the ability to look up information relating to a library, commonly referred to as documentation. You can use this help function to get information about a specific item (such as sqrt) or to look at the documentation for the entire library.

```
>>> help("math.sqrt")
Help on built-in function sqrt in module math:

sqrt(...)
    sqrt(x)

    Return the square root of x.
```

Type Conversions It is often useful to be able to convert data from one class to another. Python provides a set of numeric conversion functions for this purpose, as shown in the next group of examples. Note that the int function in the first example does not round the value 5.78 but instead "chops" off the fractional part. By contrast, the float function simply adds ".0" to the integer. In the final example, the float function converts one of the integer operands to a floating-point value. Because the float(6) operation is performed first, one of the division operands will now be a floating-point value. As a consequence, the result is also a floating-point value.

```
>>> int(5.78)
5
>>> float(56)
56.0
>>> float(6)/4
1.5
>>>
```

Variables and Assignment Statements   So far, we have seen how to carry out simple computations using the Python environment and the built-in numeric classes. To construct more complex programs, we will need to be able to store values for use at a later time. In Python, a variable is a named reference to a data object. This means that variables themselves do not contain object values but rather contain references (sometimes called pointers) to the objects. Names in Python, called identifiers, are case sensitive, must start with an alphabetic letter, and can be of any length. Names such as Dog, dog, and dOg are all different according to the Python rules.

To create a variable, you place an identifier on the left-hand side of an assignment statement. Assignment statements consist of a variable, the assignment operator (=), and a right-hand-side expression. Once the expression is evaluated, the resulting object will be used as the value of the variable—in other words, the variable will refer to the object. Asking the Python environment to evaluate a variable will return the data object referred to by that variable. An error will occur if the variable does not exist.

The first statement shown below creates a variable named `count` and associates it with the integer value 25. Figure 1 shows the variable as a box holding an arrow (a reference) to the data object 25.

```
>>> count = 25
>>> count
25
>>> counter

Traceback (most recent call last):
  File "<pyshell#32>", line 1, in -toplevel-
    counter
NameError: name 'counter' is not defined
```

The next assignment statement extends this idea by taking an existing variable, `count`, and then adding 1 to it. This new result is then "reassigned" to

Figure 1   *Variables hold references to data objects*

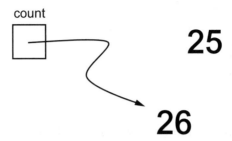

Figure 2   *Assignment changes the reference*

the variable count. Figure 2 shows that the reference for count now points to the data object 26.

```
>>> count = count + 1
>>> count
26
>>>
```

We can use a sequence of assignment statements to perform more interesting calculations. In the example below, we first assign values for the length and width of a rectangle. We can then calculate the area of the rectangle by multiplying those values together.

```
>>> length = 5
>>> width = 6
>>> area = length * width
>>> area
30
>>>
```

We can perform several assignment operations simultaneously by using the Python assignment statement. In this case, variables and values must be listed in the order we would like them to be used. For example, we could rewrite a portion of the previous calculation so that it uses simultaneous assignment:

```
>>> length,width = 5,6
>>> area = length * width
>>> area
30
>>>
```

Built-in Collection Classes

In addition to the primitive numeric classes, Python provides a number of very powerful collections. A collection is a group of data values that are placed into

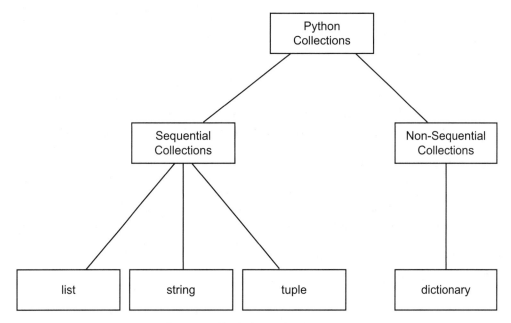

Figure 3   *The Python collection classes*

some type of organizational structure. Figure 3 shows the Python collection classes as they appear in relationship to one another. It is important to understand how each collection differs from the others and where each can be properly used.

Sequential Collections   Sequential collections–strings, lists, and tuples–allow programmers to store multiple data objects together in a structured manner. As the name implies, the data is kept in linear order with respect to one another. In addition, all sequential collections provide a common group of operations while maintaining distinct differences from the other sequential collections.

Strings   Strings are sequential collections of characters. Literal string values are delimited by quotes. Three different quoting styles can be used: single, double, and triple. As shown below, triple quoting allows a string to bridge across the end of a line.

```
>>> 'dog'
'dog'
>>> "house"
'house'
>>> "don't"
"don't"
>>> '''This is a triple quoted string
```

```
that can break across a carriage return'''
'This is a triple quoted string\nthat can break across a
carriage return'
```

As summarized in Table 1, a number of operations can be used on any Python sequence. Indexing allows access to a specific item in the collection by specifying an index value. The index value, which is enclosed in square brackets, indicates the item's position in the sequence. The indices in a sequence start with 0 and go up to $n - 1$, where n is the number of items in the string, called the length of the string. For example, in the string "house", "h" is at position 0, "o" is at position 1, and "e" is at position 4. Even though we are able to access a single character, a string is considered to be an immutable collection. That is, individual characters within the string can be accessed but cannot be changed.

```
>>> myname = "David"
>>> myname[3]
'i'
>>> myname[3] = 'X'

Traceback (most recent call last):
  File "<pyshell#56>", line 1, in -toplevel-
    myname[3] = 'X'
TypeError: object does not support item assignment
>>>
```

In addition to indexing, sequential collection classes provide several other simple, but useful operations. Concatenation (+) builds a string by combining two strings together. Repetition (*) builds a string by concatenating multiple copies of a string to itself. The length function (len) returns the number of

Table 1 Operations on Any Sequence in Python

Operation Name	Operator	Explanation
Indexing	[ ]	Access an element of a sequence
Concatenation	+	Combine sequences together
Repetition	*	Concatenate a repeated number of times
Membership	in	Ask whether an item is in a sequence
Length	len	Ask the number of items in a sequence
Slicing	[:]	Extract a part of a sequence
Iteration	for	Iterate over each item in a sequence

characters in the string. Remember that the indices of a string called s will run from 0 to len(s)-1. Finally, the membership operator (in) checks whether a specific character is part of a string. The session below shows four of these operations in action. Note that Python will always default to using single quotes for strings unless otherwise needed (for example, if a string contains a single quote, it will be double quoted).

```
>>> "dog" + "house"
'doghouse'
>>> yourname = "Franklin"
>>> yourname
'Franklin'
>>> "Franklin"*3
'FranklinFranklinFranklin'
>>> yourname*3
'FranklinFranklinFranklin'
>>> len(yourname)
8
>>> 'F' in yourname
True
>>>
```

Two other operations, slicing and iteration, offer powerful means to manipulate sequences. The slice operator, the colon in brackets ([:]), allows you to extract a subsequence by providing the starting and ending positions of the items you want in the result. It will return the subsequence consisting of all items from the starting position up to, but not including, the ending position. For example, "Hello"[0:1] returns "H". "Hello"[0:0] returns an empty string. In addition, if you leave out the starting or ending position, the slice operator will default to starting with the first character or including up through the last character.

```
>>> yourname
'Franklin'
>>> yourname[0:0]
''
>>> yourname[2:5]
'ank'
>>> yourname[:5]
'Frank'
>>> yourname[4:]
'klin'
>>>
```

Iteration over a sequence means that you can "visit" each item in the collection, starting with the first item and moving through to the last item. The *for* operator provides our first look at a structured statement. That is, a collection of statements, also known as a block, will be executed as the iteration operator moves through the sequence. In Python, all of the statements in a block are indented to the same margin to indicate that they are to be executed together.

In the following example, we will iterate over each character in the string referenced by yourname. The variable achar initially refers to the value of the first character (F), then to the value of the second character (r), and so on. For each character, the statements inside the *for* statement will be executed. In this case, we will print each character.

```
>>> for achar in yourname:
...        print achar

F
r
a
n
k
l
i
n
>>>
```

In addition to the string sequence operations, strings provide a "library" of other methods that programmers can use for string processing. (Recall that methods are operations that can be applied to an object.) Table 2 shows a representative sample of these functions.

Pay careful attention to the syntax for invoking methods that belong to data objects. This syntax, often referred to as dot notation, joins the object name

Table 2   Methods Provided by Strings

Method Name	Use	Explanation
center	astring.center(w)	Returns a string centered in a field of size *w*
count	astring.count(item)	Returns the number of occurrences of *item* in the string
ljust	astring.ljust(w)	Returns a string left-justified in a field of size *w*
rjust	astring.rjust(w)	Returns a string right-justified in a field of size *w*
upper	astring.upper()	Returns a string in all uppercase
lower	astring.lower()	Returns a string in all lowercase
find	astring.find(item)	Returns the index of the first occurrence of *item*
split	astring.split(schar)	Splits a string into substrings at *schar*

and its method by using a period. For example, the command `yourname.center(20)` can be interpreted as "ask the `yourname` object (a string) to perform its `center` method and pass it the value 20 as the number of characters for the field size." You will encounter this syntax in many different places as you learn more about object-oriented programming.

The following session shows a few of these methods in action. The `upper` and `lower` methods simply return a string with all alphabetic characters transformed to uppercase or lowercase. The `center`, `rjust`, and `ljust` methods allow you to create a new "blank-padded" string, in which blanks are added to the original string until it reaches a specified width. This ability is particularly useful for string formatting within a column. The `find` method searches for an occurrence of a particular character or group of characters, returning the index of the starting location for the matching characters in the string. Finally, the `split` method is very useful for processing textual data. It takes a string as an argument and returns a list of substrings, where the split character is used as a division point. By default, a space will be used as the split character. At this point, we encourage you to start your Python interpreter and try working with all of these methods on your own.

```
>>> yourname.upper()
'FRANKLIN'
>>> yourname.center(20)
'      Franklin      '
>>> yourname.find("k")
4
>>> yourname.split("k")
['Fran', 'lin']
>>> "The quick brown fox".split()
['The', 'quick', 'brown', 'fox']
>>> phrase = "The quick brown fox"
>>> phrase.split()
['The', 'quick', 'brown', 'fox']
```

Lists   In the last three examples from the previous section, the results took the form of a collection known as a list. Lists are sequential collections consisting of zero or more Python objects. They are written as comma-delimited values enclosed in square brackets. The empty list is simply written as [ ]. As with any other values in Python, asking the interpreter to evaluate a list will simply return the list itself.

```
>>> [3,"dog",5.75,46]
[3, 'dog', 5.75, 46]
>>> []
[]
>>>
```

Strings are homogeneous structures because each item in the structure is the same type of object—a character. Lists, by contrast, are heterogeneous—they can be composed of any kind of object. Our example list includes two integer values, one floating-point value, and a string.

Because lists are sequences, all of the sequence operators described previously for strings can be applied to lists as well. The concatenation and repetition operators build a new list by joining the original lists together. Indexing returns a particular item in the list. As with strings, indices start at 0. Finally, slicing returns the part of the original list corresponding to the starting and ending index values; as before, the slice goes up to, but does not include, the ending index value.

```
>>> yourlist = [3,"dog",5.75, 46]          #The original list
>>> yourlist + [43,"house"]                #Concatenation
[3, 'dog', 5.75, 46, 43, 'house']
>>> yourlist*2                             #Repetition
[3, 'dog', 5.75, 46, 3, 'dog', 5.75, 46]
>>> yourlist[2]                            #Indexing
5.75
>>> yourlist[1:3]                          #Slicing
['dog', 5.75]
>>> len(yourlist)
4
```

Earlier, we said that strings were immutable collections, in that you could not change individual items within the string. This is not true for lists: The assignment statement can modify list elements. Thus lists are mutable collections, in that they can be changed. The following example shows an assignment statement modifying the item at index 2 in the list yourlist. Figure 4 shows the resulting list as a collection of references to data objects. Changing an item in the list simply changes the reference stored at that position.

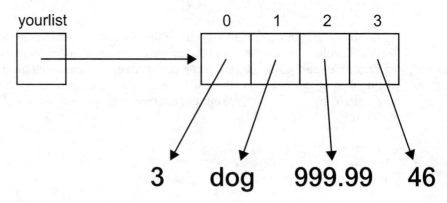

Figure 4   *A list is a collection of references*

Table 3   Methods Provided by Lists

Method Name	Use	Explanation
append	alist.append(item)	Adds *item* to the end of a list
insert	alist.insert(i,item)	Inserts *item* at the *i*th position in a list
pop	alist.pop()	Removes and returns the last item in a list
pop	alist.pop(i)	Removes and returns the *i*th item in a list
Sort	alist.sort()	Modifies a list to be sorted
reverse	alist.reverse()	Modifies a list to be in reverse order
del	del alist[i]	Deletes the item in the *i*th position
index	alist.index(item)	Returns the index of the first occurrence of *item*
count	alist.count(item)	Returns the number of occurrences of *item*
remove	alist.remove(item)	Removes the first occurrence of *item*

```
>>> yourlist[2]=999.99
>>> yourlist
[3, 'dog', 999.99, 46]
>>>
```

Like the string class, the list class provides a number of built-in methods, which are described in Table 3. Examples of their use can be seen in the following sessions. Pay careful attention to the syntax used when calling and applying methods to objects.

The `append` method adds a new item to the end of a list. As a consequence, the length of the list will increase by 1. The `insert` method, by contrast, allows you to place a new item into the list at a particular index position. Items already in the list will be shifted to make room for the new item.

There are two forms of the `pop` method. The first simply removes and returns the last item in the list. After this operation, the list is changed in that it is now shorter. The second form provides an index position for `pop`. In this case, the item specified by the index will be removed and returned. The remaining list is again shorter. The `remove` method is similar to `pop` in that an item will be taken out of the list. In this case, however, you specify the item itself, not the position. Asking to remove an item that does not appear in the list will result in an error. Two additional methods, `sort` and `reverse`, reorder the items in the list.

```
>>> yourlist=[3,"dog",5.75,46]
>>> yourlist
[3, 'dog', 5.75, 46]
```

```
>>> yourlist.append("house")
>>> yourlist
[3, 'dog', 5.75, 46, 'house']
>>> yourlist.insert(1,9999)
>>> yourlist
[3, 9999, 'dog', 5.75, 46, 'house']
>>> yourlist.pop()
'house'
>>> yourlist
[3, 9999, 'dog', 5.75, 46]
>>> yourlist.pop(2)
'dog'
>>> yourlist
[3, 9999, 5.75, 46]
>>> yourlist.sort()
>>> yourlist
[3, 5.75, 46, 9999]
>>> yourlist.reverse()
>>> yourlist
[9999, 46, 5.75, 3]
>>> yourlist.remove(5.75)
>>> yourlist
[9999, 46, 3]
>>>
```

Tuples A tuple is a heterogeneous sequential collection that cannot be modified; that is, a tuple is immutable. Tuples are written as comma-delimited values enclosed in parentheses. All of the predefined sequence operations can be used with tuples.

```
>>> yourtuple=(30,"cat",6.75)
>>> yourtuple
(30, 'cat', 6.75)
>>> yourtuple*3              #Repetition
(30, 'cat', 6.75, 30, 'cat', 6.75, 30, 'cat', 6.75)
>>> len(yourtuple)          #Length
3
>>> yourtuple[:2]           #Slicing
(30, 'cat')
>>> yourtuple[1]            #Indexing
'cat'
```

The most important difference between lists and tuples is that tuple items cannot be modified. In the preceding tuple, although we can use indexing to retrieve the item at position 1, we are not allowed to assign a new value to that location. If we try, we get the following error (the same error mentioned with strings earlier):

```
>>> yourtuple[1]="horse"

Traceback (most recent call last):
  File "<pyshell#117>", line 1, in -toplevel-
    yourtuple[1]="horse"
TypeError: object does not support item assignment
>>>
```

You might wonder why tuples would be useful, given that they appear to be so similar to lists. One way to answer this question is to think about what kinds of data you might want to represent in a collection. If the collection consists of items that could change over time, a list might be the appropriate structure. For example, a list of exam scores for a particular student might make sense because we may need to modify a score due to a grading error. Conversely, the student's name, in (lastname, firstname) form, might be better stored as a tuple because we typically would not want to modify any part of it. Using tuples allows a programmer to protect data so that it cannot be inadvertently changed by a later part of the program.

Dictionaries   Dictionaries are nonsequential collections of associated pairs of items, where each pair consists of a key and a value. This key-value pair is written as key:value. A typical example might be the association of Social Security number keys with name data values, such as "555-66-7777":"Fred Flintstone".

Dictionaries as a whole are written as comma-delimited key-value pairs enclosed in curly braces. The empty dictionary is represented by { }. For example, we could build a dictionary of office numbers for computer science faculty by evaluating the following Python assignment statement. In this case, we are using the name as the key and the associated office as the data value.

```
>>> officenums={"David":319,"Brad":321,"Kent":315}
>>> officenums
{'Brad': 321, 'Kent': 315, 'David': 319}
>>>
```

Dictionary entries are not stored in any particular order. In fact, in the preceding example, the first pair added is actually the last pair shown. Like the other collections, dictionaries provide a set of built-in methods, listed in Table 4. The following session shows these methods in action.

Because the dictionary is a collection of key-value pairs, we may want to know all of the keys or all of the values used in the dictionary. The keys and

Table 4   Methods Provided by Dictionaries

Method Name	Use	Explanation
keys	adict.keys()	Returns a list of keys in the dictionary
values	adict.values()	Returns a list of values in the dictionary
items	adict.items()	Returns a list of key-value tuples
get	adict.get(k)	Returns the value associated with *k* and *None* otherwise
get	adict.get(k,alt)	Returns the value associated with *k* and *alt* otherwise
in	key in adict	Returns *True* if *key* is in the dictionary and *False* otherwise
has_key	adict.has_key(key)	Returns *True* if *key* is in the dictionary and *False* otherwise
del	del adict[key]	Removes the entry associated with *key* from the dictionary

`values` methods will return lists containing the keys and the values, respectively. These lists can then be used just like any other list (or any sequence, for that matter).

```
>>> officenums.keys()
['Brad', 'Kent', 'David']
>>> officenums.values()
[321, 315, 319]
>>> officenums.items()
[('Brad', 321), ('Kent', 315), ('David', 319)]
```

To retrieve a value from the dictionary, we use the `get` method. This method takes a key and returns the associated value. If the key does not exist, `get` will return nothing. In the first example below, we try to get the value associated with the key `'Walt'`; because this key does not exist, the prompt is immediately returned with no value.

An alternative form of `get` allows you to specify a value to be returned if the key is not present. In the example below, we supply the string `'No Entry'` as a return value in the case that the key is not present in the dictionary. Because `'Walt'` is not present, `'No Entry'` is returned.

We can also use an indexing-like syntax to retrieve a value associated with a given key. As with indexing, we place square brackets around the index. This dictionary access style can be used to add more items to the dictionary, as shown in the final examples below.

```
>>> officenums.get('David')
319
>>> officenums.get('Walt')
>>> officenums.get('Walt','No Entry')
```

```
'No Entry'
>>> officenums['David']                    #Indexing-like retrieval
319
>>> officenums['Steve']=317                #Indexing-like insertion
>>> officenums
{'Steve': 317, 'Brad': 321, 'Kent': 315, 'David': 319}
>>>
```

1.3 Output

In the preceding discussion, our results were "printed" by the interactive Python environment as the result of method evaluation. This is the default behavior for the Python interpreter; it shows the result of the last evaluation performed.

By contrast, in our very first programming example, we used a print statement to direct Python to show something on the screen. The print statement takes a comma-delimited line of values, evaluates each one, and then prints the values on a line, separating each from the other by a single space.

```
>>> print 3,6.75,"dog"
3 6.75 dog
>>> x=3
>>> y=4
>>> name='David'
>>> print x,y,name,x+y
3 4 David 7
>>>
```

1.4 Input

Input statements allow us to ask the user to enter data that we can then store for use at a later time. In Python, the input statement allows you to include a prompt that will be printed so that the user knows what type of value to enter. The result of the input statement—that is, the value entered by the user—can then be used in an assignment statement. For example, the first statement below shows an input statement on the right-hand side of an assignment statement. The variable on the left-hand side, inval, refers to the data object entered by the user. In this case, the prompt appears and the user enters 34.75. A reference to the data object 34.75 is then stored in the variable inval. Evaluating inval shows that the input has been successful.

```
>>> inval = input("Please enter a value ")
Please enter a value 34.75
>>> inval
34.75
>>>
```

Note that the input from the user will be evaluated first. As a consequence, users can enter expressions as well as values. For example, if we use the same input statement but enter an arithmetic expression, 7*3, the assigned value is the result of the multiplication operation. In other words, the input expression, 7*3, is evaluated and the result is used in the assignment statement.

```
>>> inval = input("Please enter a value ")
Please enter a value 7*3
>>> inval
21
>>>
```

Here is a larger example program that takes some input, does some computation, and returns some output.

```
#Program to compute cost of gas purchase

gallons = input("Please enter the number of gallons: ")
price = input("Please enter the cost per gallon: ")

cost = gallons * price

print "Your purchase is",cost
```

Here is a sample execution of the program:

```
Please enter the number of gallons: 13.5
Please enter the cost per gallon: 2.50
Your purchase is $ 33.75
>>>
```

These input statements work well for most data. However, because the statement evaluates the input from the user before it assigns the value to a variable, string data will not be processed correctly. If the user enters a string, that input will be interpreted as a variable name, which in turn will be evaluated and likely found not to exist.

```
>>> input("Please enter a name: ")
Please enter a name: David
```

```
Traceback (most recent call last):
  File "<pyshell#163>", line 1, in -toplevel-
    input("Please enter a name: ")
  File "<string>", line 0, in -toplevel-
NameError: name 'David' is not defined
>>>
```

To solve this problem, Python offers an alternative input function that can be used for string data. The `raw_input` function does not evaluate the input, but simply stores the raw text.

```
>>> name = raw_input("Please enter a name: ")
Please enter a name: David
>>> name
'David'
>>>
```

1.5 Files

Instead of allowing the user to enter data interactively, we can prepare an input data file ahead of time and then read our input from the file. Likewise, instead of printing our output to the screen, we can create an output file that stores the results of the program execution. Both of these files will be text files—that is, files filled with characters. In addition, like all other data, files, once opened, will be objects in Python.

In Python, we must open files before we can use them and close files when we are done with them. Table 5 shows the functions that can be used to open and close files. For example, to open a file called `data.txt` we would apply the open function as shown below:

```
>>>fileref = open("data.txt","r")
>>>
```

This function will return a reference to a file object that can be assigned to a variable. In this case, the variable `fileref` is used in the assignment statement so that `fileref` now holds a reference to the file object.

Table 5   Opening and Closing Files in Python

Method	Meaning
open(filename,'r')	Open a file called *filename* and use it for reading. This will return a file variable.
open(filename,'w')	Create a file called *filename* and use it for writing output. This will return a file variable.
filevariable.close()	File use is complete.

When we are finished with the file, we can close it (put it away) by using the close method as shown below:

```
>>>fileref.close()
>>>
```

Now, suppose we have a text file called spider.txt that contains the following data:

```
The itsy bitsy spider went up the waterspout;
down came the rain and washed the spider out;
out came the sun and dried up all the rain;
and the itsy bitsy spider went up the spout again.
```

We can use this file as input to our program by opening the file and assigning the result to a file variable called infile. In this program we will "read" each line of the file and convert it to uppercase before printing. Because text files are sequences of lines of text, we can use the *for* statement to iterate through each line of the file. Each line is then converted to uppercase using the string method upper().

```
#Create an uppercase itsy bitsy spider

infile = open("spider.txt",'r')

for aline in infile:
    newline = aline.upper()
    print newline

infile.close()
```

The following output will be printed to the screen:

```
THE ITSY BITSY SPIDER WENT UP THE WATERSPOUT;
DOWN CAME THE RAIN AND WASHED THE SPIDER OUT;
OUT CAME THE SUN AND DRIED UP ALL THE RAIN;
AND THE ITSY BITSY SPIDER WENT UP THE SPOUT AGAIN.
```

We can also write the output to a file instead of printing it to the screen. To do so, we need to open a new file as an output file and then replace the print statements with calls to the write() method.

```
#Create an uppercase itsy spider output file

infile = open("spider.txt",'r')
outfile = open("upspider.txt",'w')

for aline in infile:
    newline = aline.upper()
    outfile.write(newline)

outfile.close()
infile.close()
```

In addition to the *for* statement, you can use three read methods to get data from the input file. The `readline()` method reads one line of the file and assigns it to a string variable. This method returns the empty string when it reaches the end of the file. The `readlines()` method returns the contents of the entire file as a list of strings, where each item in the list represents one line of the file. It is also possible to read the entire file into a single string with `read()`. Table 6 summarizes these methods, and the following session shows them in action. Note that each time we reopen the file so as to start at the beginning.

Table 6   Reading and Writing Methods

Method	Description
filevar.write(astring)	Add *astring* to the end of the file. *filevar* must refer to a file that has been opened for writing.
filevar.readline()	Returns the next line of the file with all text up to, and including, the newline character.
filevar.read()	Returns the entire file as a single string.
filevar.readlines()	Returns a list of strings, each representing a single line of the file.

```
>>> infile = open("spider.txt","r")
>>> aline = infile.readline()
>>> aline
'The itsy bitsy spider went up the waterspout;\n'
>>>
>>> infile = open("spider.txt","r")
>>> linelist = infile.readlines()
>>> linelist
```

```
['The itsy bitsy spider went up the waterspout;\n', 'down came
the rain and washed the spider out;\n', 'out came the sun and
dried up all the rain;\n', 'and the itsy bitsy spider went up
the spout again.\n']
>>> infile = open("spider.txt","r")
>>> filestring = infile.read()
>>> filestring
'The itsy bitsy spider went up the waterspout;\ndown came the
rain and washed the spider out;\nout came the sun and dried up
all the rain;\nand the itsy bitsy spider went up the spout
again.\n'
>>>
```

1.6 Conditional Structures

This section explores how Python implements the control structures. Python supports three variants of an *if* statement that can perform both simple and multi-way selection.

if Statement

An *if* statement allows a programmer to execute some part of a Python program only if some condition is true. The Python *if* statement uses a Boolean expression to decide whether to execute a block of statements or to skip them. Recall that a block of statements is a sequence of statements, all of which are indented the same number of spaces. When typing a block of statements in the Python shell, you must press the return key two times to tell Python you are done with the block.

```
>>> number = 8
>>> if number % 2 == 0:
...     even = True
...     print "The number ", number, " is even."
...
The number  8  is even.
>>>
```

In the preceding example, Python evaluates the Boolean expression number % 2 == 0. If the expression evaluates to True, the variable even is assigned the value True, and the program prints out "The number <x> is even." If the expression evaluates to False, the two indented statements are skipped. Remember that in Python, indentation is significant. Also notice that the Boolean expression ends with a colon. Whenever you see a colon, you know that the next block of statements will be indented.

if-else Statement

Python also supports an *if-else* statement. In an *if-else* statement, Python uses a Boolean expression to decide which of two possible blocks of statements to execute.

```
if temperature <= 32:
    print "Today is a cold day."
    print "Sitting by the fire is appropriate."
else:
    print "Today is a nice day"
    print "How about taking a walk?"
```

In the preceding example, the Boolean expression `temperature <= 32` is evaluated. If the temperature is less than or equal to 32 degrees, then the message "Today is a cold day. Sitting by the fire is appropriate." is printed. If the temperature is more than 32 degrees, then the message "Today is a nice day. How about taking a walk?" is printed. The important idea to take away from this example is that Python will evaluate only one block of statements.

if-elif-else Statement

Python makes multi-way conditionals easy to write by using an *if-elif-else* statement.

```
if temperature <= 32:
    print "wear your winter coat"
elif temperature <= 60:
    print "wear a light coat"
elif temperature <= 80:
    print "wear a T-shirt"
else:
    print "time to go swimming"
```

In the preceding example, the Boolean expression `temperature <= 32` is evaluated first. If the expression evaluates to `True`, then the message "wear your winter coat" is printed. If the expression is `False`, Python continues and evaluates the Boolean expression provided in the next `elif` clause. Python evaluates the Boolean expression after each `elif` clause until either it finds one that is `True` or it reaches the `else` clause. In the example, the only time the `else` clause would be evaluated is when the temperature is greater than 80 degrees.

Boolean Expressions

In Python, Boolean expressions are composed of comparisons that may be connected by the Boolean operators *and, or,* and *not.* Table 7 defines the behavior of these operators.

Table 7　Boolean Operator Behavior

Operator	Output
x and y	If x is false, return x; otherwise, return y
x or y	If x is false, return y; otherwise, return x
not x	If x is false, return 1; otherwise, return 0

When evaluating expressions to test for `True` or `False` values, Python uses the rule that any nonzero number or non-empty sequence evaluates to `True`. The number zero, the empty string, or any empty sequence evaluates to `False`.

Here is a simple example using `and` in a Boolean expression:

```
if temperature <= 32 and precipitating:
    print "Let it snow, let it snow!"
```

This example includes two Boolean expressions. `temperature <= 30` and `precipitating`. To print "Let it snow, let it snow!", both expressions must evaluate to `True`. Python also lets us write the preceding statement as `temperature <= 32 and precipitating == True`. This approach is perfectly legal because `precipitating` is a Boolean variable, and this form makes it very clear that we want the value to be true. The statement is usually easier to read when the `== True` part is omitted, however.

The next example also includes two Boolean expressions, but only one of the conditions must be `True` for the message "Stay indoors today" to be printed.

```
if temperature <= 32 or precipitating:
    print "Stay indoors today"
```

When evaluating a Boolean expression, Python uses a technique called *short-circuit evaluation*. With short-circuit evaluation, Python looks at only as many clauses as are necessary to decide whether the Boolean expression is true or false. In our first example, if the temperature was 42 degrees, Python would not bother to evaluate the expression `precipitating == True`. No evaluation is necessary because the *and* condition requires all its clauses to be `True` for the expression to be true. Similarly, if the temperature is 20 degrees in the second example, Python would not evaluate the `precipitating == True` condition: Only one clause of an *or* condition must be true for the entire expression to be true.

Finally, let's look at one example using the *not* operator. The statement

```
if 32 < temperature and temperature < 212:
    print "temperature is between freezing and boiling"
```

is equivalent to the statement

```
if not ( temperature <= 32 or temperature >= 212):
    print "temperature is between freezing and boiling"
```

Python supports a very natural way to express the "betweenness" of a temperature:

```
if 32 < temperature < 212:
    print "temperature is between freezing and boiling"
```

Like mathematical expressions, Boolean expressions incorporate the notion of precedence. In Python, *not* has the highest precedence, *and* comes next, and *or* has the lowest precedence. Just as with mathematical expressions, you can use parentheses to enforce any order of operation you desire. The following example shows how *not* takes a higher precedence over the operators *and* and *or:*

```
>>> not True and False
False
>>> not (True and False)
True
>>> not False or True
True
>>> not (False or True)
False
```

1.7 Looping Statements

Python provides two mechanisms for writing loops: *for* and *while*. The *for* loop, as you have seen previously, iterates over all items in a sequence. To create a count-controlled loop, you can create a sequence using the `range` function. The `range` function takes one, two, or three integer parameters.

- `range(N)`
- `range(start,stop)`
- `range(start,stop,step)`

Let's look at some examples of the range function in action:

```
>>> range(10)
[0, 1, 2, 3, 4, 5, 6, 7, 8, 9]
>>> range(-10)
[]
>>> range(2)
[0, 1]
```

By default, range produces a list of integers starting at 0 and containing as many numbers as specified by the parameter. As a consequence, the last number in the list will always be one less than the number given in the parameters.

```
>>> range(10,15)
[10, 11, 12, 13, 14]
```

If you do not want to start with 0, you can pass range a starting number and a stopping number. The stopping number is not included in the list, however. For example, if you really want the numbers 10, 11, 12, 13, 14, and 15 included in your list, you should pass the range function stop+1.

```
>>> range(1,10,2)
[1, 3, 5, 7, 9]
>>> range(10,101,10)
[10, 20, 30, 40, 50, 60, 70, 80, 90, 100]
>>> range(9,-1,-1)
[9, 8, 7, 6, 5, 4, 3, 2, 1, 0]
>>>
```

The third parameter to range allows you to specify a step—that is, a count-by parameter. You can think of this step parameter as a way to tell range to produce a list of numbers from start to stop counting by step. The step parameter is also useful if you want to go backward. To go from a larger number to a smaller number, you must specify a negative step.

Count-Controlled Loops with *for*

Let's look at an example of a count-controlled *for* loop that adds the numbers from 1 to 10:

```
>>> sum = 0
>>> for i in range(1,11):
...     sum = sum + i
...
>>> print sum
55
```

What if you want to sum the first 1 million numbers? While you can certainly use the `range` method to create a list of 1 million numbers, that effort seems wasteful. To help you when you need to create large ranges, Python provides a function called `xrange`. The `xrange` method works exactly like `range` except that it produces the numbers for the list just when you need them. In Python, an object that produces the results you want just when you need them is called a *generator*.

```
>>> x = xrange(10)
>>> print x
xrange(10) # x is a generator that acts like a list
>>> x[1]    # Get the first element of x
1
>>> x[9]
9
>>> for i in x:
...     print i
...
0
1
2
3
4
5
6
7
8
9
```

while Loops

In Python, a *while* loop has the following form:

```
while <boolean expression>:
    statement 1
    statement 2
    . . .
```

The statements inside a *while* loop are executed repeatedly until the Boolean expression evaluates to `False`. The Boolean expression is reevaluated each time the block of statements is executed. If the Boolean expression is `False` initially, the statements inside the *while* loop are never executed.

We can rewrite our counting program using a *while* loop to implement a count-controlled loop as follows:

```
>>> sum = 0
>>> i = 1
>>> while i <= 10:
...     sum = sum + i
...     i = i + 1
...
>>> print sum
55
>>> print i
11
>>>
```

This example illustrates a very common *while* loop pattern. Here we assign a value to a variable that ensures we will execute the body of the loop at least once. After that, the loop continues to execute until the loop condition evaluates to `False`.

The next example illustrates the use of an event-controlled loop to read and sum numbers. Python reads numbers from the keyboard until the number entered is less than zero. When the user enters a number less than zero, it sets the variable `done` equal to `True` to indicate that the loop can stop.

```
>>> done = False
>>> sum = 0
>>> while not done:
...     x = input('enter a number: ')
...     if x < 0:
...         done = True
...     else:
...         sum = sum + x
...
enter a number: 6
enter a number: 11
enter a number: 22
enter a number: 5
enter a number: -1
>>> print sum
44
```

A *while* loop is also useful for reading from files. In the following example, we open a file and make a priming read from the file. The body of the loop prints each line of the file in turn and then reads in the next line.

```
>>> dat = open('test.dat')
>>> line = dat.readline()
>>> while line:
```

```
...       print line
...       line = dat.readline()
...
1 1 1
1 2 3
1 3 5
2 1 5
2 2 3
2 3 1
3 1 1
3 2 3
3 3 5
>>>
```

One very important thing to remember about *while* loops is that if you make a mistake, you can create a loop that will go on forever. This is called an infinite loop:

```
sum = 0
i = 1
while i <= 10:
    sum = sum + i
```

The preceding example shows an infinite loop. Creating an infinite loop is a common mistake that is made by many beginning programmers. In this case, the problem is that we did not increment the loop variable i. As a result, Python will continue executing the line sum = sum + 1 forever.

Nested Loops

Just as you can put one *if* statement inside another *if* statement, so you can also put one loop inside another loop. Let's go back to our file-reading loop. Suppose that you wanted to print the average of the numbers on each line of the file. The following Python program does just that:

```
dat = open('test.dat')
line = dat.readline()
while line:
    nums = line.split()
    sum = 0.0
    for n in nums:
        sum = sum + int(n)
    avg = sum / len(nums)
    print "Average = %5.3f" % (avg)
    line = dat.readline()
```

Type in this example and save it to a file called avg.py, and then type the data from the previous file example into the file test.dat. When you run the program avg.py, here is what you will see:

```
zsh-% python avg.py
Average = 1.000
Average = 2.000
Average = 3.000
Average = 2.667
Average = 2.333
Average = 2.000
Average = 1.667
Average = 2.667
Average = 3.667
```

You can verify the results yourself by hand by computing the average for a few lines from the test.dat file.

Loops can be nested inside other loops as many times as you want. Suppose you wanted to write a program to generate the binary numbers from 0 through 7. One easy way to accomplish that task is to use a series of nested loops, as in the next example:

```
>>> for firstCol in range (2):
...     for middleCol in range(2):
...         for lastCol in range(2):
...             print firstCol, middleCol, lastCol
...
0 0 0
0 0 1
0 1 0
0 1 1
1 0 0
1 0 1
1 1 0
1 1 1
```

Although this example might seem confusing at first glance, it's really pretty easy to understand. The innermost loop controls the output that you see in the rightmost column, the middle loop controls the middle column, and the outer loop controls the first column. Notice that the output goes back and forth between 0 and 1. In fact, if you look closely, you will see that 0 and 1 are printed out in the last column each time the value of the middle column changes. If you look at the left-hand column, you will see that the middle column prints out 0, 0, 1, 1 for each value of the left column. The important thing to recognize is that the outer loops don't change the output value until the inner loops have finished all their work. Then, when the outer loop changes, the inner loops must start over again. To confirm that you understand how these nested loops work, try tracing the three loops in the preceding example, keeping track of the values of `firstCol`, `middleCol`, and `lastCol`.

1.8 Defining Functions

In Python, you can write a program just by typing Python expressions one after the other. If you save all of those expressions to a file, you can run that file of expressions as a program. However, it is often a good idea to break a large problem into several smaller problems. The way that you break up a large program into smaller parts is by writing functions.

In Python, functions are simply another kind of object. Functions have names just like other kinds of objects, but in addition to a value, functions have behavior. For example, `math.sqrt` is a function, and Python is perfectly happy to share that fact:

```
>>> math.sqrt
<built-in function sqrt>
>>>
```

When we don't put parentheses after the name, Python tells us that the object is a function. However, because functions also have behavior, we can call them (by adding parentheses to the name) and ask them to perform some work for us:

```
>>> math.sqrt(9)
3.0
>>>
```

When we define a function in Python, we are simply creating a new data object and defining the behavior of that object. The syntax of function definition looks like this:

```
def function-name(parameter, parameter, ...):
    statement 1
    statement 2
    statement 3
    ...
    return object-to-return
```

As we would expect, the function has a name and some parameters. Parameters enable us to communicate information to the function that it needs to do its job. For example, when we ask `math.sqrt` to compute the square root of something, we must tell this function which number we want the square root of.

When a function has completed its work, it may return a value. A return value is how the function communicates with its caller. Typically the last line of the function will be a *return* statement, specifying one or more values to return to the caller. If no *return* statement appears in the function, the function returns the value `None`.

As a first example, let's look at a function that requires no parameters and has no *return* statement:

```
def writeBox():
    print "...................."
    print ".                  ."
    print ".                  ."
    print "...................."
```

 # start of Program

```
print "A Box:"
writeBox()
print "Box has been drawn."
```

Type in this program as a text file, save it as boxTest.py, and then change to the directory containing the Python file you just saved. When you execute the file, you get the following result:

```
$ python boxTest.py
A Box:
....................
.                  .
.                  .
....................
Box has been drawn.
```

Notice that there is a difference between writing a function using a *def* statement and calling the function in a program later. By writing a function such as the `writeBox` function, we have essentially extended the Python language. You can use the functions that you write in just the same way that you can use `range`, `open`, and `math.sqrt`.

Passing Parameters

Python passes parameters by reference. Because variables in Python are themselves references, however, changing the value of a parameter inside a function has no effect outside the function. Let's look at a simple example of a function that has parameters:

```
>>> def functest(a,b):
...     a = 2 * b
...     print "a = ", a
...     print "b = ", b
...
>>> x = 3
>>> y = 7
>>> functest(x,y)
a =  14
b =  7
>>> x
3
>>> y
7
>>>
```

Even though the function changed the value of a inside the function to 2*b, the value of x outside the function did not change. Figure 5 illustrates the

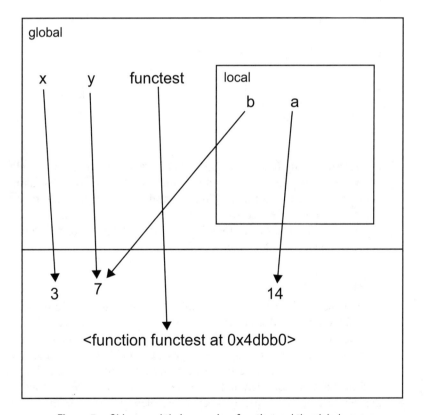

Figure 5 *Objects and their scope in a function and the global space*

relationship between variables defined locally within a Python function and variables defined in Python's global environment. The figure depicts the state of the program just after Python executes the statement a = 2 * b. The box with the label "Local" indicates the variables that are local to the function functest. The variables outside the box are the global variables, including the variable functest, which refers to a function object at address 0x4dbb0.

Because lists are mutable objects, you must be careful when passing a list as a parameter. If the *contents* of the list are changed, those changes will be reflected in the calling environment. Nevertheless, we cannot change the list to a whole new list, as shown in the next example:

```
>>> def functest(list1,list2):
...     list1[2] = 7   # Change list contents
...     list2 = [7,8,9] # Reassign to new list
...     print "functest: list1 = ", list1
...     print "functest: list2 = ", list2
...
>>> x = [1,2,3]
>>> y = [4,5,6]
>>> functest(x,y)
functest: list1 = [1, 2, 7]
functest: list2 = [7, 8, 9]
>>> x
[1, 2, 7]
>>> y
[4, 5, 6]
>>>
```

As shown in Figure 6, the change we made to the third element of x, known as list1 in the local environment of functest, was maintained even after the function returned. While x and list1 still point to the same list object, the object pointed to by the third element of the list has changed. Conversely, reassigning the value of list2 caused list2 to reference an entirely new list object but left y unchanged.

Scoping Rules

After perusing the preceding examples, you may be wondering, "What are the rules for finding and accessing variables in the Python environment? What if I want my function to have access to a variable in the global environment? What if I want my function to change the value of a variable in the global environment?"

When a function is called, a new environment—also called a scope—is created for the function. Any parameters of the function are assigned values inside the newly created scope. To keep track of variables and their values, Python uses three simple rules:

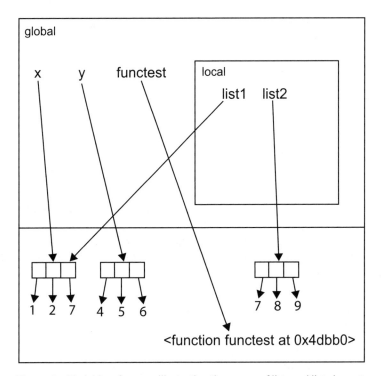

Figure 6 *Variable references illustrating the scopes of lists and list elements*

1. Python searches up to four scopes to find the reference for a particular name: (1) the local environment; (2) the enclosing function environment (if any); (3) the global scope; and (4) the built-in scope. This first rule is known as the "LEGB rule."

2. When you make (*assign*) a variable inside a function, rather than just *use* a variable in an expression, Python always creates or changes the variable in the local scope.

3. The `global` declaration allows you to circumvent rule 2.

Let's look at a couple of examples that illustrate these rules. First we consider a simple example where a function accesses a variable that is defined outside the local scope of the function:

```
>>> x = 7
>>> def functest(a):
...     a = a + x
...     print a
...
>>> functest(3)
10
```

Now let's look at what happens when we make an assignment to a variable x inside the function:

```
>>> def functest2(a):
...     x = 9
...     a = a + x
...     print a,x
...
>>> functest2(3)
12 9
>>>
```

In this example, rule 2 came into play. Because we assigned a value to x in the function, a new variable named x was created inside the function.

Sometimes assigning a value to a variable inside a function that shadows a variable in the global scope can have confusing consequences. Can you guess what will happen in the next function?

```
>>> def func2(a):
...     a = a + x
...     x = 11
...     print a
...     print x
...
>>> func2(9)
Traceback (most recent call last):
  File "<stdin>", line 1, in ?
  File "<stdin>", line 2, in func2
UnboundLocalError: local variable 'x' referenced before
assignment
```

Because we used x in the expression a = a + x, you might have thought that Python would use rule 1 to locate x in the global scope. However, because a function must be defined before it is used, Python always knows which variables will be assigned values inside the function's scope before it is called and it reserves names in the local scope to account for those assignments. Because each name is reserved but does not have a value yet, Python finds the name in the local scope but generates an error.

If we really, truly want to change the value of a variable in the global scope, Python allows us to do so—but first we have to tell Python to use the global version of the variable by including the global keyword. The next example illustrates modifying a global variable from inside a function.

```
>>> x =7
>>> def functest3(a):
...     global x      # Tell Python to use the global x
...     x = 11
...     a = a + x
...     print a,x
...
>>> functest3(9)
20 11
>>> x
11
```

Return Values

Although Python allows us to modify variables in the global environment from inside functions, doing so is not good programming practice. A much better approach is to write a function that returns a value. The return value of the function may then be used in an assignment statement for a variable in the global scope, such as x = math.sqrt(y). Here it is clear that the modification of x is intentional. In Python, functions can return one or more values using the *return* statement. The *return* statement actually performs two important tasks: It tells Python which values the function should return, and it tells Python to leave the function. Let's look at an example of a function that returns a single value:

```
>>> def isEven(n):
...     if n % 2 == 0:
...         return True
...     else:
...         return False
...
>>> e = isEven(3)
>>> e
False
>>> e = isEven(104)
>>> e
True
```

Beginning programmers sometimes forget that a *return* statement causes Python to leave the function. Here's a simple example that illustrates what *not* to do:

```
>>> def badReturn():
...     print "hello"
...     return True
...     print "returned True"  # Will never execute!
```

```
...
>>> print badReturn()
hello
10
>>>
```

Once the Python interpreter executes the *return* statement, the rest of the function is ignored.

One nice advantage that Python enjoys over some other languages is that a function can return multiple values. For example, suppose we wanted to write a function that returned a pair of factors (a,b) for a number x, such that $a * b = x$. We accomplish that task in Python by having the function return a tuple of values:

```
>>> def findFactors(x):
...     d = 2
...     while d <= (x/2):
...         if x/d * d == x:
...             return ((x/d),d)
...         d += 1
...     return (x,1)
...
>>> findFactors(99)
(33, 3)
>>> findFactors(17)
(17, 1)
>>>
```

When Python returns multiple values, it is a simple matter to assign those values to separate variables:

```
>>> f1,f2 = findFactors(54)
>>> f1
27
>>> f2
2
>>>
```

1.9 Using Objects

Throughout this chapter, we have explored examples that used some of Python's classes—namely, strings, lists, and dictionaries. In this section, we talk more concretely about a more advanced class.

Turtle Example

One enduring object in introductory computer science is the turtle, which was first invented as part of the Turtle Graphics package for the LOGO programming language. In this section, we look at Python's version of the turtle. A turtle is an object that can go forward or backward, or left or right. The turtle's tail is dipped in ink and may be up or down. When the turtle moves and its tail is down, it draws a line. When the turtle moves and its tail is up, it does not draw a line.

Python comes with a built-in turtle in the `turtle.py` module. Let's explore what we can do with this turtle object. The first step we must take before we can have a turtle do anything interesting is to create one. To create a turtle, we call the *constructor*. The constructor always has the same name as the class. The next two lines show how to import the turtle module and make a new turtle:

```
>>> from turtle import Pen as Turtle
>>> yertle = Turtle()
>>>
```

If you try out this example, you will get a window like the one shown in Figure 7. The first line of the example includes a Python *import* statement. An *import* statement tells Python to load a module containing some advanced functionality—in this case, the module containing the Turtle class. Python

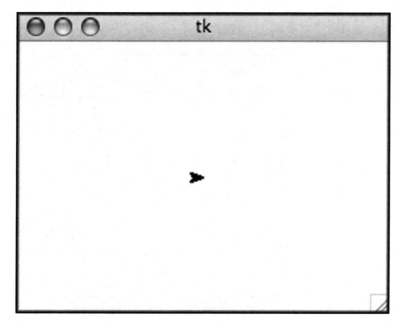

Figure 7   *A simple turtle graphics window*

comes with many modules, including those for math, network access, database access, graphics, and image processing. If every module was loaded automatically whenever Python was run, it would take a very long time to start and waste a lot of system memory. The *import* statement allows us to use only the modules we need when we need them.

The second line of the example illustrates the use of a constructor to create a new Turtle. After calling this constructor, we have a Turtle object named yertle that is waiting to do whatever we ask it to do. An arrow on the screen represents the turtle. It shows us both the current position of yertle and the direction in which yertle is headed.

When we want an object to do something for us, we call one of its *methods*. Turtles have four simple methods: forward, backward, left, and right. Let's combine some of these methods to have yertle draw a simple spiral (see Figure 8):

```
>>> for distance in range(0,200,2):
...     yertle.forward(distance)
...     yertle.right(90)
...
>>>
```

This example illustrates some important concepts to remember about using objects. First, for the turtle to draw this pattern, it must remember several

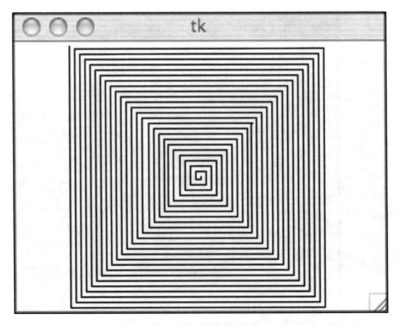

Figure 8 *A spiral pattern drawn using Python's turtle graphics*

things. It must remember whether its tail is up or down. It must remember its position in the window. It must remember the direction it is pointing. We call these things that the `Turtle` must remember its state. Inside the `Turtle` class, we use instance variables to remember the state. In the next section, we will look at how a class is implemented in Python and see how instances of the class remember those important details.

Before we leave this section on using objects, let's look at one more example that shows what you can do with turtle graphics in Python. This program uses many of the features of Python you have read about in this chapter. The Python language supports recursion, which this example uses to draw a fractal called a "ternary tree." We won't show you what the output looks like—type in the program and try it yourself.

```
From turtle import Pen as Turtle
def ternaryTree(size,factor,t):
    if size >= 1:
        for i in range(3):
            t.forward(size)
            ternaryTree(size*factor,factor,t)
            t.backward(size)
            t.right(120)
t = Turtle()
ternaryTree(75, 0.5, t)
```

1.10 Defining Classes

Now that we have used some Python classes, we are ready to write our own class in Python. A class is a template for an object. As an analogy, you might think of a class as a factory that creates instances of objects.

Defining a Person Class

Let us define a class that represents a person with a first name, a last name, and a telephone number. The minimum level of functionality we would expect from an instance of this class is that a person could tell us his or her name and phone number. In addition, we will see how to write a constructor and how to write a method that allows us to print out a person in an easy-to-read way. Here is a complete Python class definition for a person:

```
class Person:

    def __init__(self, firstName, lastName, phoneNo):
        self.firstName = firstName
        self.lastName = lastName
        self.phoneNo = phoneNo
```

```
    def getFirstName(self):
        return self.firstName

    def getLastName(self):
        return self.lastName

    def getPhoneNo(self):
        return self.phoneNo

    def __str__(self):
        stringRep = "First Name: " + self.firstName + "\n"
        stringRep += "Last Name: " + self.lastName + "\n"
        stringRep += "Phone Number: " + self.phoneNo + "\n"
        return stringRep
```

If you type in the `Person` class and save it to a file called Person.py, you can use the *import* statement to load the class for testing and experimenting. In the next example, we make a person and then exercise some of the methods of the `Person` class:

```
>>> from Person import *
>>> jane = Person("Jane","Jones", "444-1604")
>>> john = Person("John","Smith", "555-2705")
>>> print john
First Name: John
Last Name: Smith
Phone Number: 555-2705

>>> print jane
First Name: Jane
Last Name: Jones
Phone Number: 444-1604
>>> john.getFirstName()
'John'
>>> jane.getLastname()
'Jones'
>>>
```

Now we have much more to talk about in detail. In the first line of this example, `class Person:` declares that there is a new object called `Person` and that this new object is a class. Remember, classes are just objects that are also templates for, and can produce, other objects.

Constructor The next line of the example provides the first method. Methods are defined inside the class using the *def* statement. The first parameter in each method always refers to the object itself. By convention, this parameter is called `self`. Any operations that refer to instance variables of the object must use `self`. Any method names that begin and end with double underscores are considered special methods. For example, `__init__` is a special method that is called whenever a new instance of an object is created.

The rest of the constructor initializes three instance variables. As mentioned earlier, the instance variables of the object are all referenced using the `self` notation. In the constructor, it is clear that `self.firstName` refers to a different object than the parameter `firstName`.

Instance Variables

In Python, the convention is to initialize all instance variables for a class in the constructor. However, because Python is dynamic, this is merely a suggestion, not a requirement. In fact, any method can create an instance variable for a class by assigning a value to a variable that begins with `self`. Once created, an instance variable represents data that any method of the class can have access to.

Let's look at another simple example using our `Person` class:

```
>>> from Person import *
>>> john = Person("John", "Smith", "555-1234")
>>> john.firstName
'John'
>>> john.lastName
'Smith'
>>> john.firstName = "Harry"
>>> john.firstName
'Harry'
>>> print john
First Name: Harry
Last Name: Smith
Phone Number: 555-1234
```

In this example, notice that from the global scope we can access the instance variables of an object. In the second line, we create a new person object with instance variables `firstName`, `lastName`, and `phoneNo`. From the global scope, we can access these instance variables by using the name we assigned to the object—namely, `john`. Inside the class definition, however, we refer to the instance variables by using `self`. Notice also that although the `getFirstName` method is defined with one parameter, when we call the method we don't pass any parameters to it. The reason for this discrepancy is that Python always passes the object to the method as the first parameter implicitly.

The important point to remember is that for the object we just created, `john` and `self` refer to the same object. When we use one or the other depends on our perspective. If we are the programmer writing the class, we will use `self`. If we are a programmer using instances of the class, we will use the name created in the global scope.

Methods

Methods are the services that an object provides to the outside world. In our turtle example, we used the methods `forward`, `backward`, `left`, and `right`. Let's look at some of the methods we have defined for the `Person` class.

Accessor Methods Many object-oriented programmers dislike the fact that Python allows you to gain unrestricted access to the instance variables of a class by using the name.variable notation. A more common practice is for the class to provide accessor methods. Accessor methods are methods that you call to retrieve information about the object. Our `Person` class has three accessor methods: `getFirstName`, `getLastName`, and `getPhoneNo`. Thus there is one accessor method for each instance variable. The method names are nearly the same as the names of instance variables, except that the method names are preceded by `get`.

An accessor method simply returns the value of the instance variable. The reason that accessor methods are preferred to direct access to instance variables is that they support *information hiding.* An example will demonstrate why. Suppose that you implemented the constructor to the `Person` class so that the constructor takes the phone number as a string but internally stores the phone numbers as three components: the area code, the exchange, and the line number.

```
class Person:
    def __init__(self, firstName, lastName, phoneNo):
        self.firstName = firstName
        self.lastName = lastName
        phoneParts = phoneNo.split('-')
        self.areaCode = phoneParts[0]
        self.exchange = phoneParts[1]
        self.lineNo = phoneParts[2]

    def getFirstName(self):
        return self.firstName

    def getLastName(self):
        return self.lastName

    def getPhoneNo(self):
        return '(' + self.areaCode + ') ' + self.exchange \
                + '-' + self.lineNo

    def __str__(self):
        stringRep = "First Name: " + self.firstName + "\n"
```

```
        stringRep += "Last Name: " + self.lastName + "\n"
        stringRep += "Phone Number: " \
                     + self.getPhoneNo() + "\n"
        return stringRep
```

Using the new definition of `Person`, let's see how the object behaves:

```
>>> from Person import *
>>> susan = Person("Susan", "Smith", "505-555-1212")
>>> print susan
First Name: Susan
Last Name: Smith
Phone Number: (505) 555-1212

>>> susan.phoneNo
Traceback (most recent call last):
  File "<stdin>", line 1, in ?
AttributeError: 'Person' object has no attribute 'phoneNo'
>>> susan.getPhoneNo()
'(505) 555-1212'
```

The important thing to notice is that if the user of the object makes use of the accessor methods, the object behaves exactly as it did before. The user can continue using the methods of the person object while remaining unaware that the programmer in charge of writing the `Person` class has changed the internal workings of the class. However, if the user of the object tries to use an instance variable, he or she gets an error because the internal details of that object have been changed.

Mutator Methods A second kind of method that supports data hiding is a mutator method (also called a transformer method). Mutator methods are used to modify the instance variables of a class. To add mutator methods to the `Person` class, we would write methods called `setFirstName`, `setLastName`, and `setPhoneNumber`. Using these methods is the preferred way to change the values of instance variables in the class. For `PhoneNo`, we could write a mutator like the following:

```
    def setPhoneNo(self,phoneNo):
        phoneParts = phoneNo.split('-')
        self.areaCode = phoneParts[0]
        self.exchange = phoneParts[1]
        self.lineNo = phoneParts[2]
```

Using a mutator method allows the user of the class to provide the phone number in a natural format, while the class takes care of storing the details in its own internal format.

Special Methods   There is still one method in our original `Person` class definition that we have not explored yet: the special method called `__str__`. The `__str__` method provides a user-friendly view of the object when it is printed. When Python evaluates a *print* statement, it first determines whether the object has defined an `__str__` method. If `__str__` is defined, Python calls this method and prints the resulting string. Notice that `__str__` does not itself call `print`; instead, `__str__` constructs a string that it returns for `print` to use.

```
>>> print john
First Name: Harry
Last Name: Smith
Phone Number: 555-1234
```

At this point, you may be asking, "What will Python print if I don't write `__str__` for my class?" If we had not written `__str__` for `Person`, here is what we would see:

```
>>> from Person import *
>>> liz = Person("Elizabeth","Knutson","123-555-5432")
>>> print liz
<Person.Person object at 0x57090>
```

The result of printing simply shows you what kind of object you are printing and where that object is stored in memory. Because each object resides at a unique location in memory, the address serves to uniquely identify this particular instance. If you created two instances of `Person`, you will see that each has its own unique address.

Inheritance

Inheritance is the object-oriented principle that one class can be derived from another. In Python, we say that a new class inherits both instance variables and methods from another class by extending that class. In many cases, the derived class represents a more specific kind of object than the parent (that is, the base class). To see how inheritance works, let's derive a new class called `Student` that is based on the `Person` class we developed in the previous section:

```
class Student (Person):

    def __init__(self, firstName, lastName, phoneNo, major,
gpa):
        Person.__init__(self,firstName,lastName,phoneNo)
```

```
        self.major = major
        self.gpa = gpa


    def getGPA(self):
        return self.gpa

    def getMajor(self):
        return self.major

    def setMajor(self,major):
        self.major = major

    def __str__(self):
        stringRep = "First Name: " + self.firstName + "\n"
        stringRep += "Last Name: " + self.lastName + "\n"
        stringRep += "Phone Number: " + self.getPhoneNo() + "\n"
        stringRep += "Major: " + self.major
        stringRep += " GPA: " + self.gpa
        return stringRep
```

The first line of the example shows how we tell Python that one class extends another. The statement `class Student(Person):` says that `Student` extends `Person`. In addition to a first name, last name, and phone number, a student also has a major and a grade-point average (GPA).

The `__init__` method sets the values for the two new instance variables, but delegates the work for setting the first name, last name, and phone number to the parent class. Look carefully at the call `Person.__init__(self,firstName,lastName,phoneNo)`. Notice that when we call a method by using the classname.method name, we explicitly pass `self` as a parameter. By calling `Person.__init__`, the instance variables inherited from the `Person` class are correctly initialized for our instance of a `Student`.

Let's explore the capabilities of our new `Student` class:

```
>>> john = Student("john","smith","444-555-1212","CS","3.6")
>>> john.getFirstName()
'john'
>>> john.getGPA()
'3.6'
>>> print john
First Name: john
Last Name: smith
Phone Number: (444) 555-1212
Major: CS GPA: 3.6
>>>
```

Because Student is an extension of Person, we can apply the methods defined in the Person class to an object of the Student class. We can also call the methods defined in Student, such as getGPA, and we can print an object of class Student. Notice that the "right" version of __str__ is called automatically. A version of __str__ is defined in both Person and Student. How does Python know which one to use? Python finds the method that is the most specific. That is, if __str__ is called for a Student, Python will use the __str__ version defined by the Student class. If no version of __str__ had been defined for class Student, then Python would look in the parent class—Person in this case. Python keeps following the chain of parents until it finds the method it is seeking.

A simple example will make this point even clearer. First we will create some instances of the classes Person and Student and put those instances on a list. Then we will write a loop to print all the people on the list.

```
>>> john = Student("john","smith","444-555-1212","CS","3.6")
>>> mary = Person("Mary","Jones","123-444-4321")
>>> personList = [john, mary]
>>> steve = Student("Steve","Jobs","800-555-1234","CS","2.9")
>>> personList.append(steve)
>>> for p in personList:
...     print p
...
First Name: john
Last Name: smith
Phone Number: (444) 555-1212
Major: CS GPA: 3.6

First Name: Mary
Last Name: Jones
Phone Number: (123) 444-4321

First Name: Steve
Last Name: Jobs
Phone Number: (800) 555-1234
Major: CS GPA: 2.9
>>>
```

Classes Behind the Scenes

Understanding how Python classes work helps you understand the importance of the self variable used when writing Python classes. Figure 9 illustrates the various references that Python keeps track of in our instances of classes Student and Person.

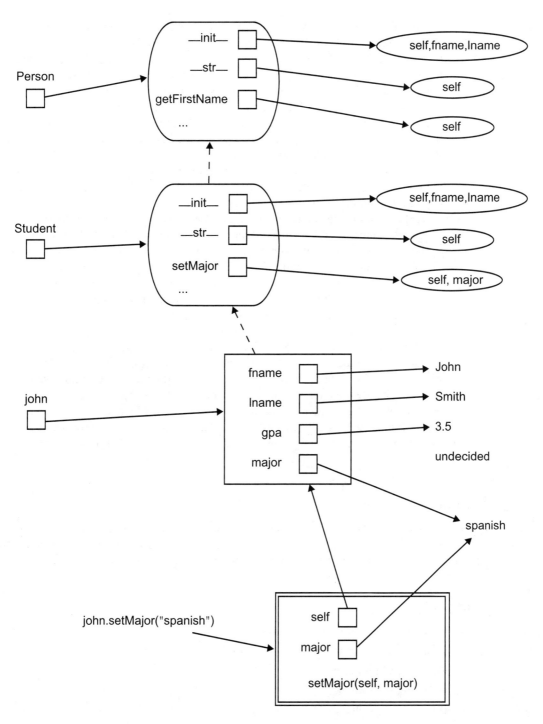

Figure 9 *A reference diagram illustrating the importance of* `self`

Assume that you have created a student whose name is John Smith. The variable that references the John Smith object is john. When you created john, this student was undecided about his major. Recently, however, he has decided to major in Spanish. Figure 9 shows the references between the various Python objects just at the point where our setMajor mutator function has updated the instance variable major from "undecided" to "Spanish." Notice that the variable john and the variable self, in the local scope of the setMajor method, both point to the same object. That object is an instance of the Student class that represents the student John Smith.

Python must take several steps to change the major, starting with the method call john.setMajor("spanish"). When Python evaluates this expression, it first determines what kind of object john is pointing to. In this case, john points to an instance of Student. Next Python tries to find the setMajor object of a Student. Because john is an instance of class Student, Python begins by searching the Student class object. Inside the Student class, setMajor points to a function object. Because parentheses appear after setMajor, Python knows to call the setMajor method. At this point Python fills in john for the parameter self, and "spanish" for the parameter major.

Next Python creates a local scope for the setMajor method call. When the setMajor method makes the assignment self.major = major, the first thing Python must do is to follow the link for self to find the student object, which, of course, is our student john. Once it locates the student object, Python finds the reference for the instance variable major. Now Python has all the information it needs to change the reference to point to the new string object "spanish".

Although this pointer tracing may seem like a lot of work to you, it actually makes Python very flexible. It also means that Python has to keep only one copy of each method, even though every instance of a class can call the methods.

Summary

Python is a modern, easy-to-learn, easy-to-use, object-oriented programming language. It combines a clear, elegant, and simple syntax with a powerful set of built-in control structures and data types. Python is ideal for beginning programmers.

Exercises

1. What constitutes a Python program?
2. What does it mean when we say that Python can be used interactively?
3. What is an interpreter?
4. What is a long integer?
5. What is integer division?
6. Compare and contrast lists, strings, and tuples.

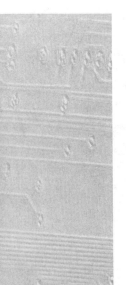

7. What does it mean to say that a collection is immutable?

8. Create a string variable that is initialized to your entire name (first, middle, and last). Write statements to do the following:

   a. Print the length of your name.

   b. Print the length of your first name.

   c. Print your last name.

   d. Print your last name followed by a comma followed by your first name.

   e. Print your name in all capitals.

   f. Split your name on the blanks (you should get a list).

9. Create a list variable that is initialized to the odd numbers between 0 and 100.

10. Create a list of 10 random numbers between 0 and 100. You will need to use the random library.

11. Create a dictionary of key-value pairs for grocery items and their prices.

12. Write a program that prints the following verse to the screen (standard output):

    Little Miss Muffet
    Sat on a tuffet,
    Eating her curds and whey.
    Along came a spider
    And sat down beside her,
    Scaring Miss Muffet away.

13. Write a selection statement that prints "Happy Birthday" if the variable `holiday` contains a 1 and "Happy New Year" otherwise.

14. Write a selection statement that prints "Happy Birthday" if the variable `holiday` contains a 1, "Happy New Year" if it contains a 2, and "Congratulations" otherwise.

15. Write a selection statement that prints the proper message based on the contents of the variable `holiday`.

    1   "Happy Birthday"

    2   "Happy New Year"

    3   "Congratulations"

    4, 5   "Happy Valentines Day"

    6   "Have a good day"

16. How does Python know to which *if* an *else* belongs?

17. Write a *for* loop that sums the integers from 1 to 10.

18. Write a *for* loop that sums the integers from -10 to -1.

19. Write a *for* loop that counts the number of lines in a text file called datain.

20. Write a *for* loop that sums the integers in a text file called datain, assuming one integer per line.

21. Redo Exercises 17–20 using a *while* loop instead of a *for* loop.

22. Write a function that takes a parameter called `heartrate` and returns `True` if `heartrate` is normal (between 60 and 80) and `False` otherwise.

23. Write a function to convert Fahrenheit temperatures to their equivalent Celsius temperatures.

24. Write a function that prints the triangle pattern shown below. Assume that the number of lines printed is a parameter to the function.

```
*
**
***
****
*****
```

25. Assume a file contains many heart rates (one heart rate per line). Iterate through the file and classify each heart rate as "normal" or "not normal." Use the function in Exercise 22.

26. Define a class `Car` that has the following information:

   a. Make, year, cost, motor number

   b. Accessor methods

   c. A constructor method to create `Car` objects with user-supplied information

   d. A __str__ method

27. Define a class `Date` that has the following information:

   a. Month, day, year

   b. Accessor methods

   c. A constructor method to create `Date` objects with user-supplied information

   d. A __str__ method

28. Define a class `Name` that has the following information:

   a. First name, last name, middle initial, title

   b. Accessor methods

   c. A constructor method to create `Name` objects with user-supplied information

   d. A __str__ method

29. Define a class called `CarPurchase` that can represent the purchase of a car. Each purchase object will have a customer, a car, and a date. Use the classes defined in Exercises 26–28.

30. Give an example of calling the `CarPurchase` constructor where a customer named Dr. Bill G. Smith bought a 2001 Honda with motor number XYZ445 for $1500. The purchase took place on March 25, 2006.

31. Show a reference diagram for the object created in Exercise 30.

32. Create a list called `PurchaseRecords` and fill it with individual `CarPurchases`, assuming that the data comes from a data file called purchases.txt (one purchase per line). Then write an iteration that will print a purchase report.

33. Create a class called `SportsCar` that extends the `Car` class. Add instance variables plus accessor and mutator methods for horsepower and the number of seconds it takes to go from 0 to 60 miles per hour.

34. Redo Exercise 32, this time including a mixture of regular car and sports car purchases.

Index